JEEZ DAD!

101 DAD JOKES SO CRINGE YOU WON'T MAKE IT PAST THE FIRST PAGE!

MATTHEW FRASER

1

ANIMALS

ANIMALS

What does a sheep say when it sees something disgusting?

Ewe

what's the difference between an indian and african elephant?

about 6500 miles.

ANIMALS

How does an elephant climb a tree?

It uses the trunk.

Why are cows great at dancing at parties?

They have all the mooooooves

ANIMALS

Did you hear about the horse that had an accident last week?

Its now in a stable condition.

What's a dogs favourite thing to play with the park?

Bark

ANIMALS

Whats the best job for a spider?

Anything with Web developing

What should you call your pet dalmation?

Spot

ANIMALS

What happened to the bear that got wet?

He was a drizzly.

What did the mother buffalo say to her son as he went to school?

Bi-son

7

ANIMALS

What's a monkey's best dance move?

The banana split

Wife: "can you leave the garbage out please?"

Dad: "Once I'm finished watching my favourite commercial sure".

ANIMALS

What do you call a nosey horse that lives next door?

A neighhhh-bour.

What does a mountain lion and a middle-aged lady have in common?

They are both cougars.

ANIMALS

What's a dog's favourite Abba song?

Poopa Scoopa

What does a snake and snoop dog have in common?

They can both rap.

ANIMALS

What do you call a dog in a rush?

A dash-hound

What's the richest animal in the ocean?

A goldfish

ANIMALS

Why did the whale blush?

It saw the ocean's bottom

How do you put the cat out?

With water

ANIMALS

What is a pig's strongest attack move in karate?

The pork chop

I had a turtle as a teacher.

He tortoise well.

13

ANIMALS

Do you know what the smartest insect is?

A spelling bee.

How come a lobster never shares anything?

Because its shellfish.

ANIMALS

What's a beaver's favorite swear word?

Dam!

Did you hear about the Horse that fell down a hill?

He couldn't giddyup.

ANIMALS

Son: "What's the smartest animal in the world?"

Dad: "your mother."

What's a polar bears favourite hobby?

Netflix and chill

ANIMALS

Did you hear about the reckless frog that got into a car accident?

His vehicle was toad away.

Why did the cat scratch me while watching TV?

I hit paws by accident.

ANIMALS

Where do sharks go on holiday?

Fin-land

18

AROUND THE HOME & FAMILY LIFE

AROUND THE HOME & FAMILY LIFE

Wife: "you are up early"

Dad: "yea, I heard you singing in the shower and jumped right out of bed"

I went to Disneyland because my kids love Donald Duck.

They were so excited when I got home and told them

AROUND THE HOME & FAMILY LIFE

Son: "Can I borrow your car today?"

Dad: *"For a million dollars sure".*

Daughter: "Your car needs washed dad!"

Dad: *"cool, well thanks for volunteering then".*

AROUND THE HOME & FAMILY LIFE

Wife: "Are you going to cut the lawn?"

Dad: "I would but I don't know where the scissors are".

Wife: "The kids are away for the weekend, I thought we could do something fun"

Dad: "ok, chess or scramble?"

AROUND THE HOME & FAMILY LIFE

Daughter: "where are the scales?"

Dad: *"Why don't you just use Instagram?"*

Son: "hey Dad, are you going to my school concert?"

Dad: *"no, the line-up looks crap".*

AROUND THE HOME & FAMILY LIFE

Wife: "What's up?"

Dad: "I guess the ceiling , the sky, the stars, the moon…"

Wife: "I think the left the oven running?"

Dad: "you better go chase after it then".

AROUND THE HOME & FAMILY LIFE

I lost my favourite football on the roof.

It's not the worst thing to happen this morning but it's definitely up there.

Wife: "which friends have you invited over for lunch?"

Dad: "My taste buds".

25

AROUND THE HOME & FAMILY LIFE

Wife: "how do I look in this dress?"

Dad: "with your eyes sweetheart"

I think my wife only finds me sexy when I make a mistake because she says *"what an ass"*.

AROUND THE HOME & FAMILY LIFE

My wife assumed I was lying when I promised to give our new puppy a silly name.

And that's when I called her bluff.

Dad: "I removed the wheels of your car".

Son: "why?"

Dad: "so now you can drive tirelessly"

AROUND THE HOME & FAMILY LIFE

I was drinking some strong coffee in my bath when I thought *"maybe I should wash some cups"*.

My wife and I have been happily married for 3 years now.

2001, 2002, and in 2005.

AROUND THE HOME & FAMILY LIFE

Wife: "the milkman hasn't come round yet".

Dad: *"How dairy?!"*

Wife: "Do you want anything for your cold?"

Dad: *"a million dollars".*

AROUND THE HOME & FAMILY LIFE

Wife: "what are you buying me for Christmas sweetheart?

Dad: "glasses"

Wife: "what, why?"

Dad: "you'll see".

Dad: "You look like what's up dawg?"

Son: "What's up dawg?"

Dad: "Not much man you?"

AROUND THE HOME & FAMILY LIFE

Son: "Did you ever play a dangerous sport?"

Dad: "yes, arguing with your mother".

Wife: "Maybe you should hit the gym, you have a dad bod"

Dad: "no, I am a father figure babes"

AROUND THE HOME & FAMILY LIFE

Wife: " I sent the kids away for the weekend"

Dad: *"are you planning on murdering me then?"*

Daughter: "where did you and mom meet?"

Dad: *"in person"*

AROUND THE HOME & FAMILY LIFE

Daughter: "I'm vegan"

Dad: "I don't read horoscopes sorry"

33

HOLIDAYS

HOLIDAYS

I went to a Halloween party dressed as the Joker but couldn't see anyone there.

It was a dark knight.

Daughter: "can we watch a scary movie since its Halloween?"

Dad: "yes, I have your birth on film somewhere".

HOLIDAYS

Why does Santa cause his elf's little helpers?

Because he doesn't want to offend anyone.

Why are witches so good at creative writing in School?

They know how to spell

HOLIDAYS

What's a ghost's favourite dessert?

I-scream.

Wife: "since its valentines, I put on some sexy lingerie"

Dad: "oh nice, where are you going?"

HOLIDAYS

What makes Santa depressed the most?

When he has low elf esteem

Dad: "I don't want a birthday cake this year"

Wife: "why?"

Dad: "because the candles will cost more than the cake"

38

HOLIDAYS

Wife: "So, what are you getting me this Christmas?"

Dad: "a massive list of the things I want"

Wife: "we need to start saving money for our next vacation"

Dad: "Good idea, can I get my credit card back then?"

HOLIDAYS

Did you hear about the ghosts in a committed same-sex marriage?

They gave each other the willies.

Why are cemeteries so noisy?

Because of all the coffin.

HOLIDAYS

Why does Dracula have no friends?

Because he is a pain in the neck.

What do you get when you throw a pumpkin from a high building?

Squash

HOLIDAYS

Why are zombies afraid of Halloween?

Because they have no guts.

Halloween is the only time of the year when I can hide in the closet, jump out and scare my wife and she won't beat me for it.

HOLIDAYS

What do you call an insect that's brought back to life?

A zom-bee

Wife: "Did you get the turkey for thanksgiving?"

Dad: "almost but then he flew away"

HOLIDAYS

What do you call Santa when he's frozen?

Santa pause.

Wife: "have you wrapped the Christmas presents?"

Dad: "Why? Where are they going?"

HOLIDAYS

What do you call a hipster vampire that vapes?

Vlad the inhaler

45

EVERYTHING ELSE

EVERYTHING ELSE

Wife: "what's on TV sweetheart?"

Dad: *"Dust"*

Wife: "Why did you buy me a gift?"

Dad: *"I thought I did something wrong".*

EVERYTHING ELSE

Dad: "You are wearing that dress to the party?"

Daughter: "yes, so?"

Dad: *"well I guess I can't give you pocket money then"*.

Son: "can I watch TV?"

Dad: *"of course you can, just don't turn it on"*

EVERYTHING ELSE

Why is real-life and Netflix the same?

If you remove all your standards, you have more to enjoy.

What do anti-vax kids love to watch on TV?

The walking dead

EVERYTHING ELSE

Girls who take about serious issues are great.

Girls who took about global issues are Greta.

I won an award for most secretive person at work.

I can't tell you how this makes me feel.

50

EVERYTHING ELSE

Son: "Can I get some advice?"

Dad: "Ask your mother, she knows everything…"

I went to the store to buy lots of toilet paper that was on special offer, *I was on a roll.*

EVERYTHING ELSE

Son: "When will you teach me to shave?"

Dad: *"just ask your mom."*

How do you get you phone drunk?

You give it screenshots

EVERYTHING ELSE

What's the capital of France?

F.

Son: "Can you help me with my homework tonight?"

Dad: "no but your mother can, she has all the answers".

EVERYTHING ELSE

I got fired as a hairdresser.

I was just not cutting it.

My wife hates my obsession with fortune tellers.

I knew it before she told me.

54

EVERYTHING ELSE

I HATE my mother-in-law.

She's always leaving the toilet seat up.

I cut off my left arm.

Now my right arm is left.

EVERYTHING ELSE

A priest recently had a bug infestation in church.

He said, "Let us spray".

Wife: "I'm making pancakes but they might be long"

Dad: "oh, I like them round".

EVERYTHING ELSE

Daughter: "what's the WIFI?"

Dad: "Ahhh, it's something that connects people all over the world through the internet".

Wife: "I got a call from an unknown number, who do you think it is?"

Dad: "Unknown since you don't know who it is."

www.ingramcontent.com/pod-product-compliance
Lightning Source LLC
Chambersburg PA
CBHW060412080526
44583CB00012B/544